A RAINBOW SHINES THROUGH CLARA

BROOKE KODISH RUTLEDGE

For my former student, Clara.
Keep flying, beautiful girl.
You taught me so much.

Copyright © 2019 Brooke Kodish Rutledge
Illustrated by Chad Thompson
All rights reserved.

The hand-drawn illustrations on this page and pages 12 and 20 were illustrated by Clara Allen.

No part of this book may be reproduced in any manner without the written consent of the publisher except for brief excerpts in critical reviews or articles.

ISBN: 978-1-61244-764-3
Library of Congress Control Number: 2019910462

Printed in the United States of America

Halo Publishing International
1100 NW Loop 410
Suite 700 - 176
San Antonio, Texas 78213
www.halopublishing.com
contact@halopublishing.com

About Clara

Clara is a nineteen-year-old young woman who lives with her parents, Jim and Kay Allen, in Corning, New York. From the time Clara was diagnosed with autism in first grade, her education focused on increasing her independence, utilizing coping skills, and improving functional communication and work-related skills before her graduation from Corning-Painted Post High School in June 2019. Clara is currently exploring all of her many options. She dreams of eventually having her own greeting card business.

For all of my current and past students who show me their beautiful colors every day.

For my fourth-grade teacher, Miss McNitt, who once wrote that she liked my writing because it came "from the heart."

For Dr. Molly Marnella, Associate Professor at Bloomsburg University of Pennsylvania, for inspiring me as a writer when she assigned us to write and illustrate a diverse children's book.

For my son, Fitz. May you always be inspired to follow your dreams.

There was once a little girl named Clara who was born to put color inside our world. Clara was like a beautiful butterfly, destined to fly and lead others over the rainbow. Clara's colors would shine on everyone she met, but sometimes people couldn't see her colors right away. That didn't stop her from flying, though.

Clara grew up with her mother and father and two older sisters named Jessica and Stephanie. From the time she was a little girl, Clara always loved driving her dad's tractor.

The years passed, and it was time for Clara to enter school. Her family began to realize that she had a hard time communicating with them. It was like she had wires in her brain that weren't connecting right.

Clara's parents took her to the doctor, but that doctor didn't believe that Clara was capable of seeing people or emotions for what they were. The doctor thought that Clara saw her mother like a chair-a lifeless object. "You will never learn to communicate," the doctor told Clara.

Clara saw her mommy as love, not a chair. That day, Clara's family felt more filled with determination than ever before. They decided to use the doctor's words as fuel. They would help Clara communicate and reveal the colors of her rainbow.

Clara's personality and ability to communicate were colors that grew and changed like a butterfly. As she grew older, Clara discovered that she had many unique abilities.

Clara was sensitive to sound, sight, smell, touch, and taste. If something triggered one of her senses, she had the magical power to stop time in her mind. In Clara's mind, the merry-go-round of the world stopped spinning, and she was left alone. It wasn't until that trigger disappeared that she would return to earth again. When Clara experienced a sensation, she would fly away to a safe place.

One day, Clara heard a fire whistle when she was at her house. She became very upset, but her family didn't know why. After the fire truck passed, they realized that Clara had heard the truck five minutes before it passed their house. Her body had sensed that it was coming long before anyone else did. After the truck passed, Clara breathed a sigh of relief and flew back down to earth. She had been in her safe place.

If a storm was coming, Clara was the first one to know about it. She would curl up in a ball on the couch, cover herself with a blanket, and try to take cover. Her body could sense the pressure of the air changing before the storm hit. It was as if Clara could fly up into the storm cloud to find out when that pressure would be released to others. Her family learned that she would always return to them after the storm had passed.

Like the change in weather that a storm creates, any change in Clara's routine could be upsetting to her. These changes were difficult for Clara to process and understand. The world did not make sense to her in moments of change, and this was when it was hard for Clara to stay on the ground.

However, Clara felt much better when she could prepare for change ahead of time. She could do this with a social story or a visual schedule of the change.

Growing up with all of these challenges, how could Clara learn to communicate? It was like Clara had forgotten the words to her favorite song. The song kept playing over and over in her mind, but she couldn't sing it yet.

First, the Allen family covered every wall in their house with pictures. These pictures were part of a program called PECS, which means Picture Exchange Communication System, that is designed to help children with autism learn to communicate.

Clara would soon learn how to use the pictures to ask for her favorite treat-fruit snacks. First, though, she spent hours pointing at the fruit snacks and crying in frustration. Then, Clara pointed to the PEC of the symbol for fruit snacks when her parents still wouldn't give them to her. Finally, Clara said, "I want fruit snacks, please," out loud to her mom and dad.

This was the first time that Clara had spoken in a full sentence, asking for something she wanted or needed.

Next, Clara began using speech-generating devices like a DynaVox to help her communicate. A DynaVox device uses an ordered grouping of pages that contains different vocabulary for the kinds of situations Clara might encounter.

Then, Clara found success with a program called Proloquo2Go. This program was easier for her to use. She could even use it on an iPad, using symbols and a human voice that spoke for her. Clara could touch pictures and symbols that appeared on the screen so that she could make requests depending on her wants and needs.

Clara's iPad began giving her a voice, especially in moments of frustration when she couldn't speak on her own.

As the grades passed in elementary school, Clara desperately wanted to shine her colors for the other students in school to see.

But how could Clara relate to other students at school if she couldn't talk to them? Clara had many favorite shows and movies. Her life ran in her mind like a movie script. She would repeat some of her favorite lines when she was upset to calm herself down. Clara liked to say, "Relax, you're cool."

When someone or something was funny, she would say, "Silly, Stew!"

Clara fiercely wanted others to hear her voice even though she couldn't tell them what was wrong.

Clara called her sixth-grade teacher "Kodish." Kodish heard Clara speaking and wanted to channel her voice through these lines by repeating them back to her. Sometimes they would spend a half hour working on a math lesson together, and Clara would start speaking in full sentences the entire time. If a problem was hard for Clara, she would start to repeat her movie and show lines to cope with the situation, but she would keep working, as long as Kodish repeated these lines back to her. This often calmed Clara down, helping her realize that the people around her heard her.

Clara also loved to communicate with her friends through her artwork. She used her iPad to take pictures of anything and everything. She took pictures of people and eventually learned to ask them first, "Can I take a picture of you?"

Later, Clara would be found sitting and looking at her pictures. In those moments, she had a smile that lit up the room. Clara's world was in pictures.

Clara was famous for making her mark on the school blacktop by drawing Disney characters in brightly colored chalk. You knew Clara had been there if you saw her perfect chalk sketches of Mickey and Minnie Mouse. This was another way that Clara found to express herself. She beamed when others walked by her artwork after recess or going to their busses and said, "Clara's been here."

Clara would soon become known in the school district for her artwork. She won awards at the annual student art show at the Corning Museum of Glass.

Clara went on trying to teach those around her with her personality and the colors she could shine on their lives. She wanted to feel that she belonged. She wanted her friends, teachers, and family to see all of her colors.

Clara took great pride in helping Kodish decorate the school for Autism Awareness month in April. Many of her friends joined a "Peer Buddies" club to spend time with Clara and her classmates. Kodish tried to plan activities where Clara's colors could shine brightest. They would dance to some of Clara's favorite songs, play jump rope, fly kites, draw on the sidewalk, and go bowling. Clara was a puzzle mastermind and could often be found piecing together a puzzle with one of her friends or a staff member.

It didn't take Clara's friends long to realize that if they were patient with her and accepted her differences, they could have fun together just as friends do every day. Kodish would look around and see how Clara's joyful spirit and sense of humor would color the room with happiness.

One day in a classroom full of her peers, her music therapist, Mrs. Schlosser, played one of Clara's favorite songs on her guitar, "Somewhere Over the Rainbow." Clara's voice filled the room as she sang every word, shining her colors on each person there. Clara's voice left everyone else speechless.

Kodish felt like she had been taken on a ride over the rainbow, transported on Clara's wings. Clara was a butterfly following the path of a rainbow, and the rainbow led to a beautiful treasure.

That treasure is a world of acceptance for autism: the treasure of all of the colors that Clara brings to this world. So many of her friends and teachers in the room that day found her treasure and saw a beautiful rainbow.

Do you look for rainbows after a storm? We can all learn so much from Clara and from others with autism if we look for their treasures. Clara's personality and love for life shine so brightly if you pay attention. You can still hear her laughter if you listen when she's not around.

When life gets hard, repeat to yourself, "Relax, you're cool." It's okay to sing your favorite song in your mind to get you through the hard times. You will see the rainbow soon. The bright colors you love will reappear after the storm that you're going through right now.

Will you hear Clara's song to remind you to keep flying?

Until then, Clara will continue flying through the sky, and *somewhere over the rainbow,* she just might catch your eye.

www.ingramcontent.com/pod-product-compliance
Lightning Source LLC
Chambersburg PA
CBHW041439040426
42453CB00021B/2462